Shortcut
to the
Next Level

Shortcut to the Next Level

Michael Tan

PARTRIDGE

To order additional copies of this book, contact
Toll Free 800 101 2657 (Singapore)
Toll Free 1 800 81 7340 (Malaysia)
orders.singapore@partridgepublishing.com

www.partridgepublishing.com/singapore

Contents

Introduction vii

Chapter 1:   The learning process 1

Chapter 2:   Know the why (purpose) 5

Chapter 3:   Self-aware/self-belief 11

Chapter 4:   Goals setting/ end game 15

Chapter 5:   Self-definition 19

Chapter 6:   Leadership 23

Chapter 7:   Honest and forgive 27

Chapter 8:   Embrace change &
              embody those changes 30

Chapter 9:   Trust 33

Chapter 10: Attitude 37

Chapter 11: Don't judge others 39

Chapter 12: Fall forward not backwards 42

Chapter 13: Habits 44

Chapter 14: Caution 47

Chapter 15: Gratitude and have abundance 51

Chapter 16: The eco-system 54

Chapter 17: Time 56

Chapter 18: The negative aspect 59

Introduction

This main focus of the book is to allow readers to clearly understand that, inside of themselves, there is an even bigger giant than they themselves can imagine.

This book is not meant for the common breed, but rather for the dying breed, so now you have to decide which breed are you, the common breed or the dying breed? Before you decide, here is a point you should understand, a common breed achieves common results while dying breed have a chance to achieve uncommon results. Which kind of results are you currently having or willing to get greater result?

If you are not happy with your results or life you are getting, there is an only one thing to encourage you to do, why not change and make that change it now?

If you are hoping things would change without changing, this book is rendered useless.

This book is structured in a way is short/ compressed and easy to finish, yet it open many lights to a normal person along with examples to how a person can relate to. For maximum effectiveness of this book, it should be read a minimum of a few times, due to personal growth and different perspective, every time reading the book allows different a different light due to personal development which allows different light. Furthermore, it is short and easy to understand. If you are expecting for a short and a general view of the subject, this is the book.

These are some of the unorthodox method that I applied in my life that helped me get to the next level, and I wish, you could level up as well. I have written this book in a way is short, clear cut and easy to understand even for the average person with applications as well!

This book has been design in 18 different chapters for you to read and learn easily. Although there are 18 different chapters, it is outmost importance for you to take note that all of the chapters are important and should not be left out just because you felt that you knew about the chapter but rather take some time to read because all the chapters are inter-linked.

Disclaimer

This book is based on what I learn and how I apply these knowledge and how you might apply it to yourself. From multiple sources that educated me in this process, understanding and the most important is applying to your own life by understanding how these things fit and become part of your life! Many sources that educated me are from the books/videos and audio books that I learn from that you may and may not heard from. These Multiple sources that enlighten me such as: art of war, Brian Tracy, Brendon Burchard, Tony Robbins, Maxwell, universal laws, Warren Buffett, napoleon hill, dale Carnegie, Zig Ziglar, Lee Ka Shing, jack ma, bob proctor, Jim Rohn, ted talks and many others.

I have spent 12 years understanding my own, and spent additional 1 year of intensive studying and learning and combining all the factors and put it in a very simple and yet understanding way for the average person to understand it, but however, understanding does not mean applying it to your life. In order to make this book effective, reader have to apply it to their OWN life and imagine how things work for your life and part be of their life and not towards other people lives.

Without the help of internet, books, education and their leadership, I might not even able to level up as I may not even understand what it means by going to the next level. I am grateful for all the technology that improved significantly which allowed learning to be so accessible and even provides the additional time to think and read to ensure the efficiency of time being spent and used.

This book if however, caused you to be in any form or any way of harm or misleading you, this book/ author (as in I) and the publishers should and would not get involve in your actions.

Any names mention in the book is purely for the sake of understanding purpose, which is not to put anyone or any names at disrespect in form or any way.

Tips to note

It is essential to understand that you learn about yourself, how I learn is to read, and write down notes on pieces of paper and file them up and read them from time to time. Do not use your mind as a filing cabinet because you will forget what you have learn if you do not use them! Be a student, write them down how they apply in your life and how does it make sense to you.

If you are thinking of the reasons why this will not help you, you will be able to find it but I would encourage you to look at it in this perspective, think about how it applies to your life and not question whether it is right or wrong.

It will be wiser if you have a mentor to guide you, a mentor with some of this traits and not just anyone

1) Have a healthy relationship
2) They defines themselves who they are and not by others!
3) People whom are results orientated
4) People whom openly admit their mistakes
5) Those who rarely gets angry or pissed off

Chapter 1

The learning process

Many of us know how to learn but may perhaps miss out the learning process and could be one of the reasons why they could not get to the next level. A simple definition of the learning process is whereby how the learning takes place. The learning process takes place in 4 different levels and as it being discuss here, perhaps the reader could understand why people may not be able to get to the next level.

Learning process: happy

Learning process

1st level: know

2nd level: understand

3rd level: application (concepts)

4th level: doing

Only doing it over a period of time, it then becomes a philosophy

Take a look at the word, happy, people could spell it and read it. Great in this step we achieve the first part of the learning process called knowing.

To dive into the second level, it is important to know the meaning of the word and also people tend to relate words with similar meaning. For example, delighted and joyful. And the 2nd step has been achieved.

The 3rd step is to application. This is where most of the problem lies. People knows the word, but have no concept upon application. In order to apply the word in your life and make it part of your life and make it work in your life, concepts are required in order to achieve the 4th step.

The 4th and last step is called doing. There is no point knowing when the person does not do anything with it.

The problem lies at people understand it so well that they could put it in either a sentence or a question. But it does not mean that they have a concept or any depth of it. Example:

Question: Are you happy?

Answer: yes I am happy, I just had lunch.

Being able to put it in a sentence does not mean you have done it, it just meant that you understand it so well that you can put it in either a question or an answer. Doing it means a form of discipline action.

Only when the person knows it, understand it, applied it and does it over a period of time, it then becomes a philosophy. So it is important to beware whether the person is giving a philosophy, or an opinion and the truth is, opinion is the cheapest commodity like Napoleon

> Happiness is found on the good side of the way things are.

hill mention. You have to use your mind to determine whether it is an opinion which is of no value or is it something useful that you could apply in your life to make those changes.

A simple concept to be happy firstly, is to be thankful and grateful. Those magical words such as please and thank you seems to vanish in our modern society today. And then say it as you mean it. Be really thankful for it. Put it in this way, if you wanted to buy McDonald but McDonald was closed for some reason, even if you had the money you could not get the McDonald, perhaps have to go to another outlet instead of that particular vendor. Be thankful or grateful for those staff mending it and them opening it. Happiness is to be found on the good side of the way things are and not the way they are.

How to listen with an open mind.

> Quote: to be neutral point of view is easy once you understand it.

Many of us say we tend to listen in an open mind, but they do not know or may not be aware of how to listen with an open mind. It is important to note that if you are not able to explain to another person how you do it, you do not understand or do not know how to do it. For this instance, 2 key words that would like to be discussed. 1) Listening and hearing and 2) open mind. What is the difference between listening and hearing? And also what are the steps to listen in an open mind?

Do you know the difference between listening and hearing? And at first I thought I knew, but in fact I didn't realize the difference. If you think you know, why not stop and take 5 minutes to think about it and process and another 5 minutes to write down the difference between listening and hearing?

It's rather simple actually if you understand it, you hear with your ears and you listen with your emotion. Now do you see the difference, and have this application in your life.

Many of the people know the term of open mind, but how many of us actually knows how to attain it? Simple, because we are not able to give them a specific steps on getting an open mind and different people may have different meaning. Another possibility is that, people tend to use based on the words to understand and may mislead themselves into understanding the terms whereby actually they do not and they are unaware. To get an open mind, it is pretty simple actually, just do not accept what has been written in this book, do not reject the idea in this book and do not neglect what been wrote in this book, just have an open mind. In short, do not accept, do not reject and do not neglect the opinion of people, but rather, look at it in neutral point of view and determine whether they are constructive or destructive by using your emotions in your mind and then you decide. If it is constructive towards your goals or improvement in your health or your result, I will suggest you really study them well.

So, I hope you read this book in an open mind. The reason why is listen with an open mind is on the first chapter is because it enforces and guides you how to read with an open mind. And to read all the chapters in an open mind. Do not accept, do not reject and do not neglect what the chapters means, use your mind and your emotion to see in an objective manner how does doing it changes you or it is constructive in a manner in your blind spot whereby you are not aware of it consciously.

Please keep in mind, if any of these chapters may not be relevant to you, but,

> Open mind = do not accept, do not reject and do not neglect.

you should read because you may not know how beneficial are the chapters to you and all chapters interlinked and may miss out vital information if chapters are skipped.

Chapter 2

Know the why (purpose)

Quote: do the things you love and you will always have the energy to do those things!

Quote: the words I and my are very powerful

The why is simply the reason why you do things. What is your cause of doing and your believe? To put it in another form, what are your intentions? All you need is simply 1 reason why you do things, and it does not require a hand full of reasons. Important to take note, other people may not like your reasons but it is your reason and you of all people should know why you do it. Your reason becomes your very purpose of doing.

> Your reasons become your why and the purpose of doing things.

Many people are doing the things that we do not enjoy, such as working in a place you dislike, going out with friends you don't enjoy. Spending time and money on things you think you are enjoying but actually you are not aware why you are doing those things. Worst of all, they are awake, getting up and doing things which does not have gets you spring out of bed to get excited to do those things.

For example, why do we work? It is simply because we needed the money, but however, if you take away the money equation, do you really know why you are working? About 90% of the people work because of money so there is a question that arises Do you know what are you working for? It is easy to get trap by economic necessity and settle down on that.

Question is there a goal that you are working towards? So in order to understand what you really love doing, you got to eliminate the equation of money in the equation, what do you work for? If it is money, money has superiority over yourself. So in short, you have allowed money to supersede you, where else you are supposed to be in control of money. I believe everyone has to pay bills but the paper bills/ plastic bills have no control over you, but rather, you have the ability to decide freely what you want to do and what you do best and decide what exactly you want. You can do anything and be anything but do not cause any harm to anyone and to yourself!

> Quote: A unexamined life may not be worth living. (Jim Rohn)

> Quote: formal education makes you a living, self-education makes you a fortune (Jim Rohn)

Another personal example, I used to be a smoker for more than a decade, 14 years to be exact, and I managed to quit because of a very simple reason, do you let your pets smoke? I assume no, then why did people smoke? If you do not let your pets or your kids smoke then why people smoke? So if people tell their kids it is not good to smoke, then question arises why as an adult doing it and they know it is bad? What is the cause or reason which resort to smoking? Assuming that Ali are addicted to nicotine, so do not mind me imposing a simple question, do you see any baby smoke? Social influence may influence greatly on the decision people make unconsciously and unknowingly. But do take note that everyone are all born the same as baby, fearless and easy to express out the ideas and free from social/environment. When a baby is hungry, the baby would just cry, does not be bothered what time is it, whether is it 4pm in the noon or is it 4am, as long as the baby is hungry, the crying begins until someone feed the child. But as people grow up, social influence have manipulated some of the decision made. Conformity is a vice when people starts to mimimic or emulate people who does not know any more than ourselves. The surrounding or people may have the ability to influence you without your awareness, then learn how to define yourself which will be shared on the later chapter. Environment is like a double edge sword, environment is much more potent then heredity if the environment is not conducive for growth but it could also enhance the growth as well. Important to know that environment plays a major part so please choose the environment well.

This comes to a realization that majority of the people are doing things under social influence whether they are aware of it or they are unaware of it. It is not an issue but you can choose not to be like them! So you got to ask yourself, why do you do things? What are your intentions and reasons for doing those things?

> Formal education makes you a living, self-education makes you a fortune.

If you do not like what you do, then why are you even waking up to do what you dislike? Why not change to a job that you love? Is it that difficult to write a resignation letter, and give it time allowance for

> Environment is much more potent then heredity if the environment is not conducive for growth

both the company and yourself to find another suitable job or career that you love?

Each of us have the ability to choose and the credentials to change. People are the same whatever the religion, race, the difference is not how they look physically different but rather their philosophy and how they arrange their mind. But many of us get mixed up with choice and circumstances. A simple concept between the difference between circumstances and choice is those circumstances are those which you do not have a choice. For example: you can never choose who to be your biological father / mother. Where else choice is when you do have an option and you can choose. For example: you can choose how you treat your descendants/ family/ friends and most importantly your business and clients. You have this choice on how to treat them but we do not have a choice who is our biological parents. People forever blame their circumstances, this happens that happens, little do they know, they are the cause of the demise because we can choose how we act.

> Quote: people react to the circumstances, but rather we should learn to act.

Here is an example to assist you to relate. John and his 2 friends Kim, Peter plans to watch movie together. As they have decided that John meets up with Kim first then Peter will come by later for the movie. Upon making that decision, the 2 of them, John, Kim headed down to meet up at the discussed area. After a period of time, Ali called Peter and said that he could not come for the movie. Put yourself in John case, how would you feel and which will you choose?

1) Finger point at Ali and blame him for putting you 3 at this kind of circumstances (reacting to circumstances)

2) Or remember your intentions of meeting up with your friends to have a good time at the movie, even though Ali is not around, you still can have a good time with Kim and Peter! (acting on own intentions/ think about the good)

People can choose any of these 2 options and it is their choice. However, finger pointing and blaming does not makes you feel happy, but rather it just makes you feel your justification, it serves you no good as it brings only frustration. So choose and decide a though that does not cause any destructive

> People are subjective towards themselves and objective towards others, we should learn to be objective towards ourselves and subjective towards all others.

behavior, but a good and peaceful ones and this is the only way to happiness. People seems to know how others should conduct themselves but they do not know how they should conduct themselves. Many people are subjective towards themselves and objective towards others, we should be objective towards ourselves and subjective towards others.

We live in a cat kicking world. Many people will tend to talk behind people back, questioning their profession, talking about why things cannot work but yet why are there people just like you with hands and legs are capable of achieving unusual results? Simple, they love what they do because they understand their why. They may work for money, they work for their passion and money is not their number 1 priority. In the rat race, even if you come out first, you are still a rat. Why be the rat when you can choose not to be!

Another person opinion of you does not have to make your reality rather you create your own reality! Understand why you do things, what is your purpose, intention and the reasons why you chose it. You either choose to do what you want to do or will you let social influence to manipulate your decision making? The choice is yours and you can make a consensus choice!

Thinking is hard work that is why people often people do not take the effort and think but they would rather rely on others to think for them. Question, if thinking is difficult and people do not do it, how much do you think will the other party will help them think? Answer, not very much! That is the reason you got to think and think for yourself and not rely on others!

> Thinking is hard work, if you do not think much for yourself, how much do you think others will think for you?

Chapter 3

Self-aware/self-belief

Quote: who and what is in control of me/you?

Many people are not aware of what they are capable of doing. There is a saying, from who we ought to be, we are only half awake. It is the awakening that leads you to be more self-aware and powered with self-belief, the seed of achievement is aroused and can lead to heights of achievements you can never expect.

Are you consciously aware of the decision that you made? Are you aware of how your time and days being used? Were some of the decision made by you or were you just following the flow and hoping things will get better and change. What and how would you define yourself? And what is your life philosophy? What makes you thick and what defines you? Are you being just like everyone else or are you being yourself?

Do you know what your life philosophy is? I will share with you mine, mine life philosophy is based on the music I listen to, heavy metal and reggae, heavy metal which tells me life is hard and keep me going on, while reggae tells me, everyone are the same, all of us struggle, and emphasize others because I know life is hard while others are also faces challenges daily. The only difference between people is our attitude and how do we face challenges when they arises.

The differences is fairly simple, we look different, our skin color is different, we have different height, weight, size, age and whole lot more difference. All those difference are only base appearances! Which is based on sight.

In a higher level of thinking, in the physical aspect, we all are the same we all have hands and legs and have been using their capabilities, such as our hands to pick up things, hold and also press and ultimately we are human beings. The only difference between people is our mental attitude which is our perspective. Think about it this way, is there any person on earth who has not sleep for 1 entire year? Is there a person who has not eaten for 1 whole year? If there is such a person, please share!

This is why people enjoy the music and also they taught me many things. Music is a form of expression towards life, that's why, music is capable of sharing the same frequency of thoughts with people. Although there are different genre, but there is definitely a certain genre that you also enjoy and might not be the same as mine. But you do know the reasons why you like them.

Who and or what is in control of you?

Quote: he/she who says he can and cannot is correct

Each individual is being governed by their own self-image and each self-image is created by your own! Each individual cannot outperform their own self-image. Self-image is based on your own level of thinking and own philosophy. Only by creating and believing that self-image which has to be defined and as descriptive as you can be, the standards of the individual is increased! Believe in yourself, because many others will not believe you, if you do not believe you can achieve, then it cannot be achieved. However, if you believe you can do it, then there is a possibility that you are able to do it. No matter how people tell you that it is impossible, you have to see it for yourself.

Here is an example, for this instance, I would use Ali as a smoker and he wants to quit. If Ali wants to quit smoking but he tells Kim "I don't think I can quit because I have been smoking for a decade already." It shows that he is telling you that he could not quit simply because of the duration of how long he smokes. And from another angle, if Ali says he wants to quit and he visualizes that he manages to quit, but he doubts in himself in his own ability to quit, then Ali is just counting the days he did not smoke, and after a period of time, he will smoke again.

If the self-image needs to be formed by the thought of quitting and you visualize yourself quitting and with the reasons why you want to quit. It has to be an empowering and uplifting until driving force that pulls you in. For example, if Ali saves the money he spends on cigarette, such as $50 per week, he could actually save $200 in a month and it will be $2400 in 1 year. And Ali could use this amount for investments, buy good food for his family, or even save for a family vacation! And this is only 1 year, if to multiply by 10, 20, 30 years, how much would he save up or earn from his investments? The amount would be submental and could be a hefty sum of money just by quitting smoking or simply by putting the $50 bills to investment.

We are not able to outperform our own self-image/ self-belief, so if a person sets a rather low self-image and doubts himself, his level of attraction may not be as high as the other guy whom sets high quality of self-image. in your eyes, you may think about you becoming that star or the celebrity, but little do you know, in the eyes of others, people are looking up to you hoping they would become just like you 1 day! So why not let's set a high level of self-image so that we do not drop so far below that image you created by yourself!

Chapter 4

Goals setting/ end game

Quote: see further ahead and not what happens today only

Goal settings are one of the key factors which affects your perspective, thinking, habits and personality. Now let's contemplate, if Ali were to have a goal which is to scrape enough money for the bills, how would feel when going to work? Well, it definitely does not excite Ali to get out of bed and head to work. So what if Ali have a bigger and more specific goal that Ali is attracted to? What I mean is your end game. Big goals are those that give you a very good feeling about them if you were to have them.

End-game is what I determine by goals in long range such as what you want to become at the end of your life by putting in time frame would be 10, 20, 30 years. By saying it this way, it allows you to understand that end-game means that it will be what you choose in the end of your life? So that you are able to sacrifice everything and go for it and not drift. What is the path that you chose or have you chosen? Another way to think about is what you would like to be in the end of 10, 20, 30 years' time? What are your dreams/ ambitions? If it is blank, why not start dreaming, and think about your dream and in your

We are being affected by our own perspective.

mind, see yourself merge together with your dream! That will make you fearless!

Many people may not know what they are doing and their reasons for doing and they accuse of circumstances by saying, have to pay bills, and if you were to think about it, everyone has to pay bills, everyone has to pay taxes. But it is their awareness which is results in their goal setting by setting a poor goal. But we all do have choice do not let the person drifting be you! If you have identified what are your goals and if it requires you to acquire the skills and knowledge, get them by all means necessary.

Learning can be done by reading a book, listening to audiobooks and even watching videos and they are not only bounded by school. School is a great place to learn, do not get me wrong but, learning takes place everywhere! By knowing things, it could save you years of repair.

Once you are able to identify your end game, use SMART goals to direct your direction towards your goal.

1) S – specific
2) M – measurable
3) A – attainable
4) R – realistic
5) T – time frame

DO NOT USE SMART GOALS TO DETERMINE YOUR GOALS FIRST, your goals/end game is step 1 and SMART GOALS IS STEP 2! Do not get them in reverse! Why do I mean smart goals is step 2 and not step 1, is because a he must identify his destination first. For this instance, the profession of a pilot will be used to illustrate the example.

For example, pilot wants to move from point (A) Malaysia to point (B) New Zealand (please do note this is an example only), he has already identified his long term goal which is New Zealand and currently at Malaysia. After that using SMART goals, to break up the long distance and use short term goals to identify where is he at and how understands what are the necessary steps to do before he can reach his destination. Such as flying to Indonesia will be the 1st SMART goal, then to India, is the 2nd SMART goal, then to China as the 3rd SMART goal and so on until reaching your destination.

Goals are like a direction in your map, they give you a sense of direction and at least you know where you are heading, a north star so that you have an idea which direction to walk towards. To simplify it, goals are affecting your personality, the way you feel about yourself and self-image. Here is a point for goal, try to have a compelling goal, something that draws you into it, as compared to a lousy goal. I would use losing weight goal as it is easy for people to understand and see how it goes.

An example of a compelling goal/dreams/end game: I would like to be lose weight by exercising so I can be young, energetic and vibrant throughout my days in my life. I will have so enough energy to do those necessary things to keep me going on. And after work, still have energy to show care and concern to

> Goals give people a sense of direction.

family and even to make passionate love with spouse. Then only exercising becomes a must do list.

An example of a lousy goal: I want to lose 5kg because I am overweight. So what happens if you have lost 5kg? You will gain back the 5kg in no time! By putting a limitation such as 5kg, it becomes a short term goal! It does not have the significance to pull you into doing them!

It is important to set goals which are pulling you in first, that draws you in that you are so willing to do the necessary things to remain in that goal and to achieve that goal, it is a long range goal, something so far ahead that draws you in and makes you do those necessary things to achieve that goal and it should be done by yourself as you will have to decide which goals excites you and allows you to get up and hit it all day. Make sure the tug of war of your life is being pulled by the future and not by the past!

I believe that people who are walking towards their goal / end game, have a different perspective and meaning of life and understands that life is hard and personally for me, if only I am a little harder on myself, then just maybe, life will be easier.

Chapter 5

Self-definition

Quote: other people opinion of you does not have to make a reality of yours.

Quote: it is easy to believe that you have a problem when you actually don't have any!

We all think in different frequency, different level of thoughts and different meaning have different impact towards different people base on the same thing. This also includes twins and people from the same culture background with the same education and from the same household thinks differently due to what the person has perceived from his mind. In short, we all are unique and have different taste and different opinion about 1 same thing, which is affected by what we think and value. I do understand that the music I listen to, many people have a negative impression of them. But then, it is your own ears and you know why you enjoy so why bother about what people's opinion? That is where definition comes in. You have to understand why you do certain things and your reasons for doing and not be bothered by what others have opinion of them once you have accepted your own definition. But however, you have to define things as it is, and not place a limitation on it.

What is Love?

My definition of love is pretty simple, it is the responsibility to take care of, until it ease of existence.

At first with my faulty thinking, I thought love was a mere feeling. Something which I could not describe and it might be a feeling. But what happens if the feeling is gone? Which means to say that I was not planning to take care of my body when the feeling of love is gone? This shows I did not plan well enough to take good care of my body and it shows that I was lacking of understanding of the word because I could not describe it to another person and it stuck with me for a very long time!

> Other people opinion does not make a reality of yours

The way the idea got to my mind is pretty simple, think about it this way, and imagine you are a parent of a new born child, how long would you give that child to learn how to walk? Like how many years, days? 1 year? 2 years? 3years? 4 years? In my mind I thought no way, until that kid learns how to walk no matter how long it takes! So here is the crucial piece of the puzzle, no matter how long it takes! That's is where I finally got my answer not to place a limitation!

That is one of the reasons why people who love to do their work hardly get any time off but many people working, tents to get medical certificate (MC) or thinking of retiring just because they wanted some time off. So in order to understand what you really love doing, you got to eliminate the equation of money, what do you work for? Do you work for money or for the goals that you are walking towards and it excites you? By doing so, you will hold great tenacity and value it!

How do you define yourself? What does these words mean to you? Persist? Self-love? Love? Take some time to think about them, not by what I mean but rather what does it mean to you.

All these words can be found in dictionary, but however, to me it is a different meaning. Persist to me it just mean that I won't die. Take the idea of the worst case scenario, what could be the worst that could happen to me? Take for example cycling for this instance, what is the worst case for learning how to cycle? You know the answer, if it is just fall down, scratches, then won't die one. That is why I love heavy metal music because of the power and the lyrics in there are so empowering.

Knowing why, your reason, you understand why you are so passionate to do your work. Why you could work for 8 to 12 hours a day, 5 to 7 days a week and just keep going on and on and on. You love doing your work because work the reason you are able to reach and walk closer towards your goal, your end game, your dream. You must first define what your goal and be definite before you can start walking towards it.

Do you love yourself? Do you know why must we exercise? Do you love your body? And do you know people cause themselves to be unhappy? We all have choices to choose and we can learn to make better decision making! If you do not love yourself, and always find it hard to be alone, then it seems like you are not aware of the definition of self-love. Do understand and relate to this 1 point, if you do not love being by yourself, and always need to find someone to be with you, then what makes you think that people will enjoy being with you when you can't even tolerate your own self? If you are not able to love your body, do you think you will get a good body? We can escape from many shackles, but the shackle we can never escape from is our own body.

People always want instantaneous results with little or no effort which is impossible. Trainers devote and invest time and effort to train up just for their body to look good and to stay healthy. You can do it too. Be in harmony with your body and love what you have been given, be grateful and thankful because there are people less fortunate than you.

So here is a challenge, try to be by yourself, | A flock of a feather flock together. |
no hand phones, just you, yourself for a little walk for 15 minutes. A very simple challenge, are you up for that challenge by giving it a shot? What is the cost of this to think about it, it is only 15 minutes of your time for 1 month? If you fail doing it for a day, the month resets until you are able to achieve for a month, while walking, feel free to think about anything. Are you happy? Do you find peace within yourself? Are you capable to enjoy the moments with yourself?

Here is a question, why is it positive people are not in flocks, only a very small minority, but the majority of people are in flocks? So it is actually quite easy to be positive and embrace those changes by shifting away from the social norm, be yourself define yourself and wear it and wear it out for the rest of your life! Do not let anyone or the environment dictate your reality and capability! A flock of a feather flock together.

I remember Sun Tzu said in art of war, he mention about discipline. It is to follow orders without question, to do those necessary things that have to be done. Are you capable of making yourself do those necessary things without question and hesitation? If you are able to apply this in your attitude, for your work, exercise and your schedule then you have certainly far ahead of many others.

Chapter 6

Leadership

Quote: Whatever decision you make, you pay the price, do not let others influence your decision.

Quote: lead don't follow

Leadership in a nutshell, is rather simple, it is you are the commander, and you are supposed to bring the camels to the river and along the way, drink up water along the way until you reach your river. So from here, you understand that leadership is actually rather simple but yet many tasks to do and to think and plan. Another illustration is such as many people are sheep, lemmings, following people blindly just because they said take it, and it is good for you. The cost of ignorance is quite a high price to pay.

Another scenario, sometimes, just like in the airport car park, there are so many levels, but there are always | Ignorance is a high price to pay | some people waiting for a lot at level 1 even though there are level 2 and level 3. Why do people rather wait in level 1 for a lot for minutes or even hours rather than going up to level 2 or 3 to search for a lot when level 2 and 3 have an increase of possibility of increasing their chances right? It's funny some times, but however, it is their choice and we should not be judgmental. However, you can make a change by being a leader. 1 very simple reason to be a leader, because the very first person you have to lead is none other than yourself.

> Quote: to lead yourself, use your head, to lead others, use your heart.

Although there is many Others whom are more specialized with this topic, I would suggest that these few list are a start for being a better leader.

1) Prioritize— do what is the most important task.
2) Lay out goals – know the direction you are heading
3) Ahead – foresee what coming ahead, problems and ratify them
4) Notify key personnel – foresee replacement
5) Allowing time to acceptance
6) Head into action
7) Expect problems
8) Always point to successor
9) Daily review plans

In short, it is to PLAN AHEAD.

Many people may have unknowingly be doing so much things and yet not being happy and successful. Specifically for this purpose, prioritize is of grave important. Prioritize those of which are the most important and necessary things to do and do those most important things them first and do not proceed to the next until the job is finished.

When things does not go according to your way (murphy law), such as failing an exam, people can only do 1 out of these 3 things. 1) Finger point and Blame everything, the school, and the teachers. Example: the teacher/lecturer said this chapter not important, the lecturer did not teach this subject. The weather was too hot, too cold, and too difficult.

2) Blame yourself. If only I had studied for this chapter, if only I done this, if only I had put in a little more time for this chapter/subject. The if only arises. Blaming yourself will not do you any good, but however, it is your fault for failing. 3) Look for a solution. Think how to resolve this issue. Many people tend to blame everything except themselves and might not be your fault for things to happen. Why not start learning to look for solutions!

In order to know that it is only your fault and being able to do the necessary adjustments required within yourself, you need to understand leadership. That is a shortcut to leadership but however, leadership is much depth than that. Remember, an archer who failed to hit a bull's-eye at 100 meter target can only think within themselves what gone wrong, identify the mistake and take another shot. Other archers could have hit the bull's-eye but why not you, although we can blame it on the wind, the bows and even the arrows, likewise, all the archers were also being affected by circumstances of wind and the environment. But ultimately you were the one holding the bows and arrows. It is alright to make mistakes but at least search within yourself for the answer why you missed and resolve the mistakes. It is alright to make mistakes but learn where was wrong!

In leadership, practice deliberate and the use of praise rather than condemnation. If you were to think about it, how much would you pay yourself to use condemnation on yourself and how would you feel about it as compared to using praise. Of the 2 option, which will make you feel better and respond better to and willing to pay more to?

> Learn how to control your emotions and do not let your emotions control you!

If you do not like condemnation, what makes you think or feel others may like it? So do on others as others do onto you. If you think praise will be much more valuable than condemnation, practice deliberately on the usage of praise. Praise on every small thing, it is like the light to the plants. It is a need to spur growth!

And if you were to look at it from another perspective, how does condemnation actually do you any good? It does temporary let you feel the right to vent out your anger and frustration, but it shows that you are direction your emotions towards anger and frustration. Nothing good comes from these but it is a learnable skill to learn how to control over your own emotions and do not let your emotions control you!

Chapter 7

Honest and forgive

Quote: you can lie to the whole world, but there is someone who knows the truth, yourself.

It is easy to lie, or many people would rather use it as an excuse to get something or get away from something, but it is almost very difficult to be honest on every idea. Life is already difficult, why not just tell the truth. It is not easy and it takes a hell lot of courage. And I believe, people of your caliber have this courage. People tend to favor the lies as it is easier and becomes an excuse. How many lies did we lie? To be honest, I myself is not able to count the amount of lies which includes white lies and all other lies. Why not speak of the truth and the whole truth for 2 weeks and see how does it change you, what is the worst that could happen to you? On my opinion, only 2 things can happen to you

1) People will be laughing at you
2) People will be watching you

People who understands will be watching you because it takes a lot of courage and determination to do the things you want to do. Those who laugh at you will not understand why you do things but rather they see it in a short term

> The angry can be made happy again but the dead cannot come back to life.

perspective. They will tell you all sorts of negative information such as, it is not worth honestly, and lying allows us to get away from that moment of truth. So there are others whom might be laugh but why not you make a decision to deliberately cheer them on doing something they find it valuable to do because we all think and value things differently.

Secondly, I would like to share with you my meaning of forgive. The word forgive, to me it means that the feeling of others should be changed daily and not based on one incident carry the same baggage your entire life. Which is to completely let go and abandon of the past and the feelings and emotions should be changed daily as every day is a new day. Imagine those feelings of the past memory tied to a string and cut it away! That is easier said than done.

> Quote: an angry man can be made happy again
> but the dead cannot come back to life.

The past is the past and it is impossible to go back into the past, but it is only possible to relieve in that incident in your mind which cause you to have resentment and frustrate you. To illustrate this point, think about it from this angle, the year 2000 was gone, you and I could not rewind the clock to relive

> We should not look into the future with anxiety and fear, nor the past with agony and regret but around us with awareness.

in the year 2000, but however, in our mind, because of an event or something happened, you remembered clearly which have an impact on you! if you are able to forgive people who has done harm to you, hurt you or even cheat you, that is when you realize, many people have a past, however, if you keep looking back on the side mirror like in a car then you will never be able to focus on the windscreen.

All you need to do is to forgive. Majority of the people may have done something wrong in the past, which is not an issue, just learn what went wrong and what you're your reasons of action and change! Remember, once decided, do not look back, although many things will be forcing you to look back. If you however, choose to look back, it is hard for you to move forward. Are you aware the time when you are driving a car, once you look at your rear mirror, your focus is on the rear mirror and not on the windscreen? It is important to look at the rear mirror to check blind spots but you do not focus your attention at the rear mirror and drive it on the road right? Same perspective as for life, look ahead and not dwell into the past just because of some mistake make by people which includes you.

You will not have peace if you are still thinking about the past, and have resentment over a cause of event that alter your state of live. Only by forgiving, accepting the past and grow from it, you can understand peace. Remember, things and people changes, but some yet however there are those whom choose to remain the same ignorant as they were years ago.

> Quote: we should not look into the future with anxiety and fear, nor the past with agony and regret but around us with awareness.

Chapter 8

Embrace change & embody those changes

Quote: To change is to simply change the thinking/philosophy and the conduct changes.

Quote: yesterday was gone, you paid the price so will you let today just pass by like yesterday?

Change is a process whereby it is not easy, but adaptable by everyone. For example, if you would cross your hands, and see which thumb is on the top, change the thumb that was supposed on the top to the thumb below and how did you feel?

> Change in thinking/ philosophy and conduct changes.

Why do we change? Why things change? Why have our lives become so much better and yet at the same time, so much harder? It is simple, because we want to improve. Things are not perfect and it could be improved. Social, cultural, teaching, education, leadership, all these are some of the issues whereby it can help the society to either be constructive or destructive. People deem change as destructive as it does affect their life 1 way or another, but it is necessary to make those changes! Let's put it this way, how would you feel if the world did not change 50 years ago. To put it short, the hand phone you are using, does not even exist! Those movie theater does not exist, not to mention about heaters and air conditioning which allows us to sleep well at night!

Many of us tends to see the change and finger point where they could improve, but do nothing to help in that area together with social influence and how they talk themselves out of their dreams, they choose to remain the same. Doing the same things and with the same attitude and hoping things would change but it will not change for the better.

Just because people told them it is difficult or they think they could not achieve doing it does not mean you could not do or achieve it. Remember, all of us, male/ female are the same, we all have physical bodies and in our physical body, combined with our 5 senses (smell, taste, feel, hear, sight)

Why (for this instances, let's assume there are 2 people) is it 2 people in the same company, in the same neighborhood with the same education and with the same background could achieve 2 times the other person result? Why some are able to achieve their goals while others just doing mundane work? Why many refuse to learn and take the necessary steps to carry on with their dreams/goals/end game and ambitions and yet unaware that their attitude is not beneficial towards themselves and they think that they are always right just because it is their opinion.

How do you expect to change when you are doing the same things the same way in the same mental attitude? Change by change what you do daily, small step at a time. If you do not have a clue on where to start, why not start by doing some reading, gather more knowledge. Do some deliberate learning! It is the books that you read give you the idea and not those books that you missed reading. After that spent some time by yourself, look within yourself and how do you define yourself. Improve on yourself because, things will not stay the same.

The name of the game is result, is either you change or the results will never change. Do you think the sun will rise from the north and set in the south just for you? You know what the chances of that happening is! Things/results will not change unless something change and the change is you and it has to be done by you willingly and on your own accord!

Chapter 9

Trust

Quote: there is a season to sow, there is a season to reap, but you can't do both in the same season.

Quote: whatever you reap is what you have sown.

Are you aware that there are people who simply do not trust themselves, but rather they relying on other people to help them do decision making. In my opinion, it is alright for people to do decision making for you, but at least make sure the person is getting good results or is good in that area.

Here is a question for you to think about. Who do you think will make better decisions for you? These are these 2 options, 1) by your own self or 2) your friend? Do you trust your own decision? In the past, I always rely on others to decide for me, what to do, where to go and even what to eat. Even studies, what to study, study business, it is good for you. Everyone is bombarding you with information. Although everyone meant well for me but, it dawn upon me I wasted so much time whereby their result are just as normal as well. Because I trust the decision people made for me, I did not realize that why did I trust them? Their results were being average and they in fact I should be at blame for

> There is a season to sow and there is a season to reap, but you can't do both in the same season.

entrusting those decision when I should be thinking and deciding for myself rather than letting others decide for me. I neglected my own thinking and allowed them to do my thinking for me which was not beneficial for me.

I trusted those decision as they meant well for me but however, do they know exactly what is my dream/goal? Have you identified yours? Do not get me wrong by saying education is not important, but rather putting in this perspective whereby, have you define what are your goals? If not why you do those things that does not lead you to your goals. This was 1 of the mistakes I did in the past, and I hope you learn them well, it was a very costly price that I paid dearly in terms of both money and time.

Do you know there are people do not even trust in their own voices/ words and thoughts? Isn't there a person whom you can trust your entire life upon? Easy to find out who! Just go to the mirror and see, the answers are right before your very eyes. SELF – belief! So the question arises, do you trust yourself? If you are listening or getting advice from your friend, look at attitude at work, is he happy at work? What are his goals? Is he very capable and result orientated? How do you determine these factors? Based on his goals. Having good and big goals will have an impact on you, but also, having a lousy goal will affect you. If unsure, please re-read those chapters, self-belief and goal settings.

There are people whom do not trust themselves, if you unfortunately happen to be one of those people, allow me to ask you 1 simple question, if you are not able to trust yourself, then how is people going to trust you? Do you remember, a quote from leadership, whatever decision you make, you pay the price. You have to trust yourself, because only when you reach the end, then you can connect the dots. But it is easy to give up half way. This was a quote from Steve jobs'.

Be the person you trust by trusting yourself, only then people will trust you. And if you trust yourself, then slowly but surely, you will see the happiness that you

> Only when you reach the end, then you can connect the dots. But it is easy to give up half way.

have created. All which is internal factors rather than exterior factors.

You can find a mentor, but make sure the mentor you are finding have uncommon results, and have uncommon attitude.

> Quote: Eagles don't flock, sparrows do and become a heavy hitter

Question: education is important, but education is not only found in school, where else can you learn?

Although many of us go to school and learn but many stop learning and growing once they left school. People have no idea where to gain

> It is an unending challenge to see what will you become.

knowledge from. Education comes from everywhere, people, newspaper, internet, books and so much more. Although school enforces you to learn but however, school does not encourage lifelong learning as once the module has ended, and if you are capable of putting it on paper, you have passed the test. So a question arises, putting it on paper and applying it on your life, which is easier? On paper, just memorize the answer, you are like a photocopier. Why is it important to learn? Are you the same level as 3-5 years ago or are you improving by learning? Your standards could either remain the same which means being obsolete, or going up by learning and acquiring new skills?

Keep on learning, do not ever stop learning. Learning have to be in a deliberate manner rather than being forced. Learn those that it seem important to you and learn it because it will get you to your goals/end game!

I trust that you would keep growing and it is an unending challenge to see what you will become.

Chapter 10

Attitude

Quote: the 4As to doomsday, 1) Arrogance
2) fear of being Alone 3) Adventure of disruptive
4) Adultery

Attitude is one of the key aspect whereby it is very tricky. Attitude is actually simply putting it how do we react. This is when perception comes into play, how do we defer things that are different and how do they have an impact on us? Attitude and mindset are very similar.

Are you aware that when you and your friends watch a movie, some may think that it is a good movie while some may not think so? A same movie, with different analysis and different perception towards the same group of people watching the same show. Now why is it this way? People view issues base on experiences and they may not be wrong, but it is their perception and you have yours.

> Negativity is normal, but learn to manage them.

It is not an issue when your friends and peers said some negative stuff. Simple, the reason is pretty simple and logical if you look at this way: everyone thinks and feels differently because of how they reason it. You are who you are and they are who they are for whatever things that goes in and out of their mind. Your reasons make sense to you due to your beliefs and harmonizes with your thought. People may have an opinion of your choice but do not let their opinions affect you. Just because some random stranger tells you are crazy does that mean you are crazy? Does it sound logical to contemplate on their opinion whether is it constructive leading you towards your goal or is it destructive which stray you away from your goals.

It is important to note that negativity is normal, so is positivity but the main factor is learning how to manage the negativity. What happens if, weeds grow in your garden? You can either clean it up or it will grow up to your foot! Learn to manage those weeds by doing the necessary things and not let them grow in your garden. Learn to be at the gate of your mind to prevent anyone from dumping rubbish into your mind or allowing weeds to grow!

Do you know some people will criticize on others only but they do not even believe in their own believes. It is kind of weird

| Be at the gate of your mind! |

whereby people do not believe in themselves, but rather, they think it is impossible just because it is hard and unattainable currently at their current state or it takes too much time and they talk people out of their dreams! Why do people believe on the negative part rather than believing that they are capable of handling it? Just because it may be difficult and requires a heavy load amount of effort and time. Why not make an effort to believe something that is constructive towards yourself? It is easy to believe you have a problem but actually you do not even have any problem. It is the ignorance that we all pay, every one of us pays it in terms of time likewise so did I.

Quote: ignorance is not bliss, but it is a tragic ending

Chapter 11

Don't judge others

Quote: in order to grow up, some mistakes must be made, which includes others!

Everyone is very similar or look the same in physical sense. The majority of us have, a pair of eyes, a nose and mouth, a pair of hands and 2 legs. In physical sense, we tend to look different only due to skin color, and size difference. But however, do note that most of us is of the same, been through struggles, hardships and we all celebrated on special occasions and success.

When people are young, they needed to learn, and how learning took place was by making mistakes and wrong decision making. Many people were once lost, had made many mistakes and have a history, but if they were to keep looking back into the past just like looking at either of these side mirrors in a vehicle, will always be traped by the past and could not move forward. Do not look back, as others are also struggling for their goals, dreams. There are some who are not intending to go to their goals/dreams but do not be like them and do not judge them. They may be having some difficult times or they are just ignorant about it. It is your past experience and your knowledge because what have went into your mind that allows you to let you be who you are today and your actions and habits to be in the future.

It is also impossible to tell you how to think, rather, the only way to lead you is sharing upon how I think and depending on how you are going to relate it. Because each of us think in different frequency, so whatever applies to me may not apply to you, but however, if you are able to relate some of the case scenario, and apply it to your life and have empathy, and realize how things work and become part of your life then I am glad to share with you my friend, you have wisdom. And if you are not able to related, do not sweat it, just read it again and again and believe it or not, when you read it with a higher degree of awareness, it will show you a different perspective from the first time you read it.

We all are trap in a black box, and I would refer to as trapped in our own hell, whereby at times, we do not say or do what we actually think or come to our mind and even do what our mind tells us to do. In an instance, one of your friend is smoking at your room, and you are a non-smoker, and assume you hate the burning cigarette smell, what will you do? Would you

1) Tell your friend to just smoke outside of your place and you tell him the real reason which is you dislike having the cigarette smell in your room
2) You let him smoke in your room just because your friend is smoking while you tolerate the smell in your room that last for a couple of hours

In this case, black box is often what is required of us to do, but many of us fail to do so. Due to several reasons

1) You give in due to the reason that person is your friend
2) The stench will only last for a couple of hours.
3) Not much of a disturbance

4) You would tolerate for your friend happiness
5) Think about what might happen (fear)

Why not do what your mind tells you? It is impossible to not tell him and expect your friend to understand what is in your mind. If you are not capable of telling, then people will tend to over extend the level of their comfort zone into your property which ultimately causing you to be unhappy due to these reasons. Take back control, tell them just because they are unaware, they may not know simple. Why not just give it to them straight up?

Doing so may result in the sour of the friendship but should not you be happy that you realize that he was there for his own benefit only? Are you not glad that you have seen through him and his purpose of getting close to you? What your friends' intentions were? For their own benefit and at the cost of your happiness.

Chapter 12

Fall forward not backwards

> Quote: you can be who you want to be, stick with your principals and do not let your 5 senses and others to influence your decision!

Have you notice kids when they fall down? They get back up, only difference is they are crying while we take a longer time to get back on our feet. Where else many of us, sometimes, fall down in terms of failing, they stopped progressing. When you fall down, and you can look back up into the sky, then you can get back up!

It is alright to take breaks, not an issue to rest, but remember to get back on your feet. How many of us, tent to be rather layback just due to some issues and problem that arises? Problems can be looked at 2 different perspective.

1) Challenge (to figure it out how to resolve and face the challenge)
2) Pain in the ass (complain about problem)

It is not easy to get things done, or delegate to someone that you trust to get it done. Life is difficult. How will you choose

> Kids always get back up, but sometimes, we stay on the floor too long.

your life? It is not up to me to be judgmental/ to even decide or think for you, you have to think for yourself.

Success and failure is like either side of the coin, heads or tails. Both have to exist and impossible to exist without either result. It is one of the law referred to as (universal laws) which does not apply to you and me but it applies to everyone living on this planet.

Failure allows individual to learn much from it. What was the cause of the failure, why did it fail? How did it fail? Knowing all the cause and effect, the next try, may be better than the previous. However, life have no such thing as a guarantee because if anything can go wrong will go wrong. (Murphy law) in short, it meant shit happens.

Have you noticed when people are being pushed back against the wall, they just somehow manage to do it, miraculously they did it, they learn it and they did it!

Life is full of challenges, faced and those unknowns and even daily operations are challenges. It is all these challenges that makes life interesting, unique, which allows people to venture into the future. Life should be a fun adventure and it should never be a bore.

Chapter 13

Habits

Quote: listen to your thoughts and look at your habits.

Quote: bad habits are those that makes you feel degenerated while good habits makes you feel good

How to spot the difference between good and bad habits: good habits are those are that improves the quality of your life, while bad habits are those that are destructive towards your life

Habits are action which have been done over a period of time, which cause it to be a part of your routine and everyday action. It has been identified that if an action have been done in the course of 21 days, it has become a habit. But, for me, the time frame is about an estimate of 28 days/1 month.

Both Good and bad habits are actually bought by each individual. By doing it several times (repetition) and for a period of time and it will soon become a habit. I remember the first time when I smoke, I was coughing, degenerated and did not really understand what the purpose of smoking other than making new friends and meet new people. And even at times, in workplace, I will use smoking to take a quick "get away" from work just to stand and smoke.

And then slowly, as time passed by, I have been smoking for a decade! 10 years of smoking due to the habit of excuse of meeting new people. Even at home, I will smoke every after meal as it was the social norm to "feel good" to grab a stick after a meal.

> Both good and bad habits are bought by the individual themselves.

So it is important to be aware of the habits that you are currently having and list down the habits currently faced. If you have some bad habits which is destructive, change them. It takes a certain amount of courage, mental strength and attitude to get rid of the bad habits. But, I am very certain, that you are capable to decide which habits are those that are hindering your potential and you by all means, eradicate those habits by hook or by crook. If millions of people can do it, there is no reason why you can't!

One of the key factors that hit me was I did not listen to my thoughts and access on were they a beneficial or harmful habit. Instead of loving your own body, I was actually doing more harm to it than I knew.

The truth is, I was not self-aware of this habits eating my health and my mind away. Now that you are more aware, the mind and body should be as one, in harmony and in a good relationship. Good habits are those habits you need to hang on for your dear life, where else bad habits are those that are causing you to not achieve your goals. What do I mean by that is pretty simple, which is easier? Smoke a cigarette and do nothing for 30 minutes or take a walk of 30 minutes?

Many people will tend to choose the easier task, which is to smoke and do nothing for 30 minutes, that is simple argument, but why don't you love your body like how you loved these bad habits? That is your body given to you, under your control and was given to you at your birth right and your duty to take care of your own health and do the necessary to take care of them. Society does not demand you to have a healthy body, it has to be demanded from yourself!

It is important to emphasis that everyone has no difference other than physical appearance differences. Why is it people are able to quit while others said it is impossible to quit? It is simple, due to their self-believe and their self-awareness. In one of the quote, who and what is in control of you? Is it a miserly cigarette or whatever drugs that you need it daily? Remember, you chose to take those drugs and harm your body, it is also your duty to purge them from your own health! It must be a choice done by your own, and you must see it in your self-image that you are capable of doing so first.

Take charge, take control of your own health. Nothing is easy, only harmful things are easy after it has become a habit. Once it has become a habit, the cost is high and increase in the difficulty to purge away but it can be done. But in you I trust that you will have these abilities,

> It is your duty to take care of your own health and do the necessary to take care of them.

overcome, adapt, and succeed. I believe you can overcome any hardship that render to you, adapt any kind of torment to help improve your health and finally enjoy the success of the problems you faced based on your self-belief that you could overcome them. You love your own body, and not dependent on substances to make you feel "good" because you naturally, love and feel good about your own! If millions of people can quit and I can, there is no reason why you can't change those bad habit.

Chapter 14

Caution

Quote: Whatever course of action that you wish to undertake, please make sure it is a product of your own conclusion

Quote: what you think today will impact on what you do in the future!

Quote: Whatever action you do, there will be consequences and no one else to blame except you!

Think about your habits, it takes so much courage to stop and even more effort to get things done. Harmful things are usually

> Whatever course of action that you wish to undertake, please make sure it is a product of your own conclusion.

a quick fix on issues, but not generally on the long run. Such as smoking a cigarette, it is harmful and it does not do you any form of benefit other than making you feel degenerated, maybe that isn't how you felt when smoking but that was how I felt and how I quit smoking. But it definitely cause you monetary losses. If developed a habit of saving money, saving money comes in naturally, and if the habits of taking good care of the body, time will be invested in exercising.

There are people do not make think twice before doing any action, at times, people are doing things they are not even aware social influence have influence them. So one key issue arises, are you being influenced by these factors, social (people), environment, even your friends doing decision making for you? Or will you be the 1 who thinks for yourself despite all the influence that try to manipulate your decision making?

Remember in the habits, bad habits come easily, sleep late, playing games and even waking up late, watching television and the most important aspect, distraction! Distraction is one of the key factor whereby it causes people to be unproductive and procrastinate leaving things off.

For every action, comes a reaction (the price we pay) and do you know what comes before that? Thinking does! Have you come across your mind whereby you did something unknowingly? For example, going to office, going out with friends. In your thoughts, you have already decided that going to work will bring you an income to sustain your life. But, did you reflect on the decision, whether did it make you enjoy on your decision?

Thinking is good, but do note, things will not be done if there is no decision made! Decision have to be made and action have to be made in order to have things getting started. In my opinion, there are 2 kinds of thinking, slow thinking and fast thinking. Slow thinking tends to foresee at different aspect of views on the outcome of the result. Thinking and foreseeing what are the different aspects that might happen and what are the cause and effect scenarios. For example: smoking, causes teeth to be black due to the stain, unhealthy gums and expense on the cigarette on the long run. And not to mention, the finance consumption on the product of cigarette, put it 1 pack of cigarette is $10, and take it 3 packs a week, which was my rate which amounts to a 12 per month = $120/ month. The amount is not significant, but however, if you look at this for the long run of over the course of 10 years how much would you save? In addition, if you use this amount and do investments, a mere $120/month to invest which will bring you more freedom? A freedom of a smoke break or your retirement? You make the choice you decide. Bad habits do you no good where else good habits ensures a good and steady living.

Fast thinking is such as little cause and effect scenario. For example: smoking a cigarette, it is easy to take out from your pocket to put

> Fast thinking is like driving a car switching lanes.
> Slow thinking s more of detailed thinking and analysis.

the stick into your mouth and light it with a lighter. Super-fast and not very time consuming. Just a matter of a few seconds or minutes. Normally this kind of decision requires very little time to think about. Also just like driving a car, shifting into the other lanes.

Where else slow thinking comes from detail thinking, analysis of what are the possibility, the results, problems and issues, problem solving. A list of thinking just for a purpose, to ensure it happens and making it happen!

And decision making, usually people will tend to look at different aspect or rather the slow thinking unless you are capable on making gut judgements then could use the fast thinking. If you previously had made a bad decision which occurs you to a financial loss or a bad relationship, people will tend to use that as a reference point and get jammed by those past mistakes and tend to look into the side mirror of your life past. And in this part, you could refer to chap 12, fall forward and not backwards. That chapter is supposedly to guild you that we do make mistakes, we are meant to fall but grow from the mistakes and because of those wrong decision that you made, that allows you to grow and become the person you will become in the future. Learn what went wrong, is it the lack of caution and slowing down thinking first by doing the necessary preparations such as reading up information regarding the issue and the company, the practices, the books before making a decision.

Chapter 15

Gratitude and have abundance

Quote: Show gratitude for everything, and if you really count your blessings, you actually have abundance of it.

Quote: to be thankful for another person effort/ things for the sake of your convenience.

Quote: every blessing taken for granted becomes a curse, and those curses torment us.

People are not taught how to show gratitude towards things that helped them improve their life, and that is the reason why people tend to take things for granted. For example, a smartphone. Well, if you look at it in this perspective, a smartphone could send messages, via WhatsApp, make calls, watch videos, play game, take pictures, calendar, write notes, check e-mails, and it is like a mini computer. We tend not to show any significant signs on how this actually assist our lives but only at a bare minimum.

So in order to show how a use of a smartphone improves our lives significantly, we need to define how does these ideas actually you

> Every blessing taken for granted becomes a curse, and those curses torment us

as an individual. We would use the same example for a smartphone, in a reach into the pocket, you are able to gain access to this device which enables you to make calls to your family members, friends, peers, as and when you want, and on the contrary, your family members are able to have a direct communication with you by calling and WhatsApp in case of an emergency or when they just miss you. This allows me to save my memory in my brain, no need to remember all my contacts number! Think about how much number you got to remember smartphone did not existed. With this device of a smartphone, you are able to gain access to the internet and watch videos, download movies, and play game when you have the extra time or relaxing. If you have an extraordinary scenery, you could also use this device with you to capture the moment of even make it into a video and share it with your family and friends to share the joy with them. With the assistance of the device, I could gain access to calendar to check out the schedule and even birthday reminders also saving brain from remembering all of your friend's birthday dates all for the convenience of the user. The device also to write down notes on what to do on the to do list, furthermore, also write down what are missing stocks from home, by writing them down on the note, shopping made much more efficient and saving so much time. E-mails could also be checked in not so technology advance country with the aid of this device. Lastly all these functions are like a mini computer which allows each individual to gain access just in their reach of their pockets which is called a smartphone!

If you realize, this is just a basis of a smartphone, and not all of the functions of a smartphone was discussed as I may missed out on the applications. If you were to do it, with whatever you have, you will come to a conclusion that you have an abundance of it. Count with what you have first and define how it significantly improves your life.

Everything has an effect 1 way or another. To emphasis it, if there is no air conditioning and heaters for example, how would it affect the environment you work in? With no solution to change the temperature in the room/office, how would you be affected? Are you able to work in an extremely cold place without the help of heater? Assuming that you are capable, how efficient would you be?

Show gratitude to everything, it is because without their existence, people would not be able to utilize the product and service. Be thankful for everything, you are who you are because of your past experience and now you are able to grow from it. Could you imagine living in a country which has no air-conditioning, no fan, and no heater to alter the temperature for your preference? Be thankful for everything that has been here.

Chapter 16

The eco-system

Quote: everything is connected to everything else, what you do, will have an impact on others

Have you notice that in an organization, we rely on one another on different profession to get the job done. Organization relies on cleaners to clean the office, tele marketers to do cold calling and to generate additional potential clients, finance department to manage company finances, human resource department to administer staff and applicants with their entitlements / benefits/ compensation and even leave. Even though all these requires different school of thoughts, but all are necessary to fulfill their purpose in the organization. Without the exception of any party, all of them have to work hand in hand together along with company policy and regulations to achieve maximum effectiveness.

With different profession requires different school of thought, it is important that every different profession have certain rules and regulation upon their profession. Such as accountant, they tend to have audit to proof the transparency of the finances. Purely an example!

With different profession requires different school of thought, it is

Everyone is just as human as you and I

important that the people comply with the certain rules and regulation upon their profession. It is not meant for people to be judge them base on their paper qualification but rather their mental attitude towards themselves and how would they treat other fellow colleague/friends and even family members. Paper qualification is just a piece of paper, but the intangible, attitude, level of awareness are more of an important aspect that should treated more dedicatedly. We all should live in harmony, even though they may come from different background, different levels of educational levels, different principal of their live, but, we are still the same, all of us are as human as you and I.

Let's brainstorm this together, how Ali would feel if he were to construction a building by himself. Seems pretty huge but it can be done, but it makes absolute no sense to do so, if Ali were to do so, he needs to learn how to draw the blueprints for the building first, secondly, materials equipment's to build, and the time, resource and effort to build it all by himself! How long would it take a normal person just like you and me with 2 hands and 2 legs to build a building all by himself with the help of equipment's, blueprint and people?

Never the less, in this book, compromise the same theory, every chapter in this book is also inter-related. All is required is to utilize what you know and change what is bad. No doubt there is a possibility that there might be certain chapters that may be unclear to you, keep reading it, by doing things over and over, repetition will certainly allow you to achieve certain results and even allows you to have different light of understanding just by reading this book.

Chapter 17

Time

Quote: once the time has pass, it is gone and can never return

Quote: time is the price each of us pays for our ignorance

Time is the unknown variable, which can only be derived by a certain amount of time years you have spent in your lifetime.

Use an example of a hour glass and represent the amount of time you own which means to say your life. At the top is the future, and the bottom is the time that you spent normally referred to as your age. It is clear that from that description, it is unknown to all of us how much time you have left, but however, each individual knows how much time has been spent because we all know our own individual age.

How many people are unconsciously aware of how they spent their days and little by little, it has become their habit of doing so. They just wandering around, complaining about why people are capable of obtaining results that they dream of. And

> Time is the unknown variable which can only be derived by the amount of years you have spent in your lifetime.

little by little, their future sand has been spent unknowingly and unconsciously, the time has flown by.

The sand does not stop even when you are beaten down to your knees, or you are celebrating. The sand in our life is on a constant flowing basis that will not stop even if you could stop the sand from the hour glass.

One example: a 21 years old boy was riding a bike, or even crossing the road, just before a bus crash onto him that killed him, he may have easily more than 10 years of his life, but due to this incident, his sand at the top has been wiped out! So instead of wasting your time on the unproductive, such as complaining and whining, Let's make it to good use, due to the fact you do not know how much is left!

How have you spent your time? The sand never stops and wait for you, it just keeps going and there is no method to stop time and eventually, your time and my time will be up and it is just a matter of time! There is no escape from the sand, no matter how much money you and I have, we could not buy the extra sand! Make full use of the sand and share your wisdom with the world.

Quote: those who are fit to die, are fit to live

Be fearless upon what you have dream to do, because the sand is constantly flowing, and our hourglass only tilts when our time has ended (death). Do not let others stop you and even yourself to talk out of what you want to do. Do those things because people are not capable of looking through your eyes, do it because you see the wrong in the social norm and make improvements! Do it because you see the fault at things and how would you improve!

Get those things done because it is your duty to do so to make an improvement towards people. People do not think the same way as you, do it because you are capable. As adversity and failure are of certainty, hope and wish for more skills, wisdom, and techniques to overcome and overwhelm the problems and grow from it.

Chapter 18

The negative aspect

Do any of this will not lead to an improvement of your life and this chapter is to refresh your knowledge.

Do any of this leads to frustrations and it serves no purpose

Procrastination / delays

> Quote: if the necessary things needed to be done, why not start taking action now

The world has become such a small place with the aid of technology. Sometimes it is easy to browse through the internet, smartphones as they change our lives and make things so convenient. By using the computer, clicking and clicking, we can buy our favorite shoes, food, books online. As time goes by, things are becoming much more accessible and much more convenient until a certain point, people tend to be distracted by the internet and spent huge amount of time browsing through time after time useless and worthless videos.

Procrastination is what often we all do but are unaware of it and habits are one of the reasons. Why do we procrastinate, why do we tend to do things later rather than not taking any action? Simply because the comfort zone is making us feel comfortable and not stretching. Why only 3% of the population are earning huge amounts of money while 97% of the population are having average results?

Procrastination is one of the negative aspect. Delay and wait and things will never get done or it gets done after a long period. People often do the secondary things first as a mistake rather than doing the most important thing. Have you taken into consideration that some people in your work place, family members or friends tends to delay when things are needed to be done? For example: you have an assignment due Friday, and you come to take notice on Monday, what do you do? A rough idea on how a person may think.

1) Start by Thursday, Thursday than find out more info, do some research 1 day should can finish if I rush it.
2) Still got 5 more days, got so much time, why don't I start after I feel more like it?
3) Start doing some research, write it down on calendar on Thursday you have to summit, so that effectively on Wednesday, you could have finish the task and doing some checking of the completed work for errors and the flow of the work.

You know that the assignment needs to be done, why many people wait until the very last minute and do those things. Do it fast, finish it, and get over with it. It is certainly not easy, as even I myself while writing this book sometimes tend to procrastinate as well.

Are you aware that your mind is like an escape pod when it comes to getting things done? Our mind usually helps us by giving this option to escape by delaying such as watching videos after videos, like some senseless video. It is not easy, but it is simple, just finish the job, get the job done no matter how long or how hard or you could give yourself a time frame so after a period of time, if your still not done or tired, why not get a break/ take a walk.

By reducing the amount of time you procrastinate, you can be much more productive which ultimately increase your value.

It is alright to take a rest, it is alright if you have done what you have planned at least at the end of the very day, you know you got the things done. But at least, do those necessary things and do not over extend the time you are distracted. Things/issues will not be done or resolved unless you have delegated people to do the task or you have done it personally.

Mr. Know it all

There are some people whom referred to as Mr. know it all as they know everything. When you told them how they could improve or develop a higher degree of thinking or awareness, Mr. know it all would give his opinion, but yet his conduct is just mediocre.

It's funny some times that Mr. know it all knows is able to have a opinion of things but does not have a clue upon his own conduct. The change needs to be from inside then only the change takes place. Does it make sense that if the person, is able to change their thinking and obtain a higher level of awareness, then the way he perceive changes if not it remains the same.

Here is an example, if the house is painted in a different color, it appears to be different, might look newer, nicer colors than previously but the outlook and the structure remains the same. To make change, it has to be made internal and not the external. Only when the structures of the house has been made such as demolishing and rebuilding, rearrangement of the furnitures then only the house made a total change of interior designs and even the looks of the house changes.

Drifters

Drifters are those who just following blindly without thinking why they are following. Why are they listening and seeking for advice from people whom are unsatisfied and unsuccessful and yet thinking that they could be successful? They will not reach the mountain by drifting and will not be able to know which direction of mountain is he supposed to be heading.

Drifters maybe unaware of the choices that they decided on, it might not be in favor towards themselves. Be consciously aware of the decision that you make, are they moving you towards your goal, improvement in your health or are they simply another person agenda to help you make the decision.

Put it in perspective, let's use everyday items that all of us come in contact with such as water and ice. If Ali is like water, drifters that does not know what defines him, then in different situation, different environment, or different flask or cups, he will shape into the flask/cup. But, if Ali defines himself, such as ice, even in different environment, different flask/cup, he is still being the same him. The exact personality of him! Learn to be like ice and water, define yourself like ice and then be like water, learn to have improvement.

We are not able to drift to the top of the mountain, but however, if we being our true self, the next level you, you will experience next level of thinking and analyzing.

Complaining, whining, murmuring, gripe

This is one of the most deadly, disease and yet people are not sensitive to this toxic. It is the killer that countless people are doing it effortless while remain anger within themselves. Finger pointing, blaming, doing all these action does not lead to resolve the issue, but rather it draws so much energy from you.

Think about it, why at times, we get so pissed off. It is basically due to the infringement of your own beliefs that others has caused it. There is an alteration in your belief, such as results, expectance, which cause you to be agitated. Some example would be egoism, while walking down the street, a random stranger knocks your shoulder, at times, you will not feel nice, and tend to tell him off just because of this minor incident. Or even at times, there is a small gap on the floor when you walk pass, it caused to fall, and may blame on the construction worker that did a bad job. Did it occur that it might be due to wear and tear, and it was your fault for not being aware of it? And what is the purpose of complaining? It does only temporary self-fulfillment by letting off some steam but it is absolutely a destructive conduct and behavior.

Before you complain, I would like you to focus on this area, do not complaining about your neighbor's roof being dirty when your doorstep is dirty. Do not ever complain, and do not ever compare! How do you feel when people coming to you and complaining about you? I would assume no, so do not complain, do not finger point at anyone. It does nothing beneficial to you or to anyone. Look for solutions instead, it would be much wiser and takes more leadership to do so as well.

Mental paralysis (indecisive) and fear

The toughest decision is to make a decision and sometimes, not making a decision is also a decision. Many times, people tend have include fear and thus not being able to make a decision. Fear in any form is as good as in existence. People tend to think of what might happen, which cause them to stay put in the same situation. For example: using learning how to cycle for this instance, while learning how to cycle, I will fall down and hurt myself. The fear kicks in already, fearing to fall and getting hurt. But if you were to think further about it, that is all, just get some scratches, bruise and cuts, no big deal. They will heal up time, maybe some scars but that's about it.

Decision making is cure for this. You have to decide what it is, and make commitments to get it no matter how hard is it. Being define assist on the reasons why it could be done. Do not think about the cost, if you were to think about the cost, it will not happen. But it is important, to think about the struggles, how is it you plan to endure and keep moving forward.

Doubt

Thinking whether the idea will work is one issue, to doubt yourself with the credentials and ability is another issue. The severity of self-doubt is undeniable! Do not ever doubt yourself! People sometimes think very lowly of themselves such as not being able to do the task properly. Others may doubt your ability to work but you should never doubt yourself! Doubting yourself only lowers your self-esteem and self-confidence which shows you have a very weak self-image of yourself.

The way to overcome doubt is by being definite and define, you will value your own thinking and will be at great tenacity and shows great self-image and very self-empowering. Do not ever, belittle by your own and by others! Believe in yourself!

Resentment

Events and people from the past may hinder your performance and emotion due to incident or mishap which cause you to be dwelling over a long period of time. The person may not know it is their own fault that causes their demise. And even it is their fault, the past has been over already, no use looking your life in the rear mirror and thinking that tomorrow will be better, it is a dumb game.

The person may also not be here, it is the thought that hinders your creativity and efficiency. The past is the past and it is over, if you were to dwell on the past, just like keep looking back your past events of your life, then how are you ever going to focus on the future? Think about it and consider the facts about it.

To overcome this, you must learn how to forgive them and most importantly forgive yourself. Learn the art of not carrying the old baggage from the past events but change it daily. A person may have done wrong in the past but he may change, so can you! Learn to cut off the string attached to the old baggage, the guilt, the curse and swearing of another person. It does not do any harm to the person but it does to you!

A poem for forgive.

The misdeed of yesterday should not be mar today.

For the things he said & the things you did

Have long since passed away.

For yesterday was nothing but a trail.

From the mistakes of yesterday

Will come some noble deed.

Do not condemn the past

For it is gone with mistakes

Forget the failures & misdeeds

Why should you let your head be bowed?

Lift up your heart and eyes.

It would be my opinion to say that I believe you are much bigger than the problem itself. Is that old past hatred of yours making you narrow minded. We all make mistakes, but at least learn where are the mistakes made and rectify them and change for the better. I believe you can.

Pessimistic

The ugly pessimistic leads a very sad and ugly life. Rather than finding virtues, he finds faults. Instead of thinking and cranking ways how to resolve issues and challenges, he thinks of ways why things cannot succeed and he is contented when he does! The non-pessimistic look at the whole donut and realize there is a circle in the center while the pessimistic only sees the circle! It is always easy to find fault but it takes totally no leadership to do so, as compared to identifying the issue and try to resolve it. See the objective as a whole, and take life as a learning experience to slowly and gradually understand and look for solutions. Do you think by being pessimistic will increase your value or decrease your value?

Finding fault and making mistakes are 2 totally different issues. Mistakes are made due to miscalculations or even ignorance of the subject, however, finding fault is by only putting your time and energy to contemplate on the issues which doubt it would fail. See the good side as compared to the bad side, it certainly does not increase your value doing the bad side. People are able to forgive on mistakes in judgement, but it becomes a unforgiveable on a mistake on intent.

Bonus (money)

Money is a sensitive issue and it should be much more comprehensive. Let's start with $1, this dollar can start by buying food on the table, provides shelter for people and most importantly, money help us to make our lives better.

Take this 1 dollar as your income, how should the money be divided?

10 cents pay yourself first. You worked hard for it, you spent the time and energy working, 10 cents should be paid to yourself. Most people missed out this step as they did not pay themselves nor do they have a well throughout plan for their economics.

70 cents paid for expenses. We all need to pay for expenses for food, leisure, transportation and many expenses.

10 cents paid for loans. Placing loans on a premium is due to the fact that interests on loans way too costly.

5 cents placed being generosity. Nothing teaches character building much more effectively than being generous.

And finally the last 5 cents is have an emergency fund. At emergency times, you will depend on funds to help you get out of the dark and stormy seasons, emergency fund could perhaps provide the solution, it should be at least 60% of your 1 year income.

So this is a plan to assist you in the economic pathway, the plan may altered, you may also change to your liking, but at least have a blueprint of how are you using the dollar.

Economics plays a large part in everyone life, it is important to take note of how the dollar is being used.

Keep strict accounts upon your finances.

Summary

Do take note that this book, is not trying to tell you how to think, but rather, it is a guide that leads you to some critical information that you may not be aware. To achieve better results, things must change and what needed to change? That change required is you, because if you are hoping for a change, the environment will never change. The sun will not rise from the north and set in the south just because you hope it would change. Things will not change unless you changes and it takes leadership to do so and on my personal opinion, everyone is a leader for a simple reason. In order to be a leader, you have to lead, and the very person you have to lead, is yourself!

Many people may live their life base on habits such as a puff after a meal, what time to go to work. Notice that people often will also think for themselves and you should think for yourself too! When is the last time you think for yourself! Define yourself, define your goals, and define your objective and then commit yourself towards that decision, no matter what others say about you, whether is positive or negative, you stick to who you are and follow through. You define what you are and not based on other people opinion and criticism.

Learn to think for yourself, which is the best option for yourself. Thinking for yourself is catered for yourself and it may not be nice to others. But to achieve uncommon results, you have to be an unreasonable person. To illustrate this point, who is more important, your friends or yourself. Are your friend happiness affecting your happiness or is happiness comes from internal influences. External forces may influence you but ultimately you make that decision. Think about this perspective, you decide whether you are happy not others decide whether you should be happy! It is a choice to be happy or unhappy, you decide. People think of how things appear to be, get a higher level degree of thinking and choose to think only the good things!

The you today is just a shadow of the you in the future. And how do you interpret your future? Should it be just a blank piece of paper, or you have already identified what is your end game, your goals what your directions should be. Define what are your goals, your future are your 30 years from now! Think like monstrous hulk that big!

Everybody have the ability to take full control of their own health, body, and mind. Life is not easy and it is never easy, but however, it is simple. Be at the guard of your mind 24 hours a day and 7 days a week and take note of what goes in and out of your mind. Watch what you eat and what you are learning. Do not believe what the social norm is saying just because they are saying it but rather use your mind and analyze and think for yourself, is it a positive and constructive manner or was it destructive and stray you towards your goal? You have the credentials to take full responsibility and control over your own, and these are the criteria for a dying breed which is to grow and know.

Do take note, all the chapters are inter-related, self-belief first to believe you are capable of doing so and then take action to get those things done! Things will never get done unless you have dedicated someone capable of doing so or you have done it. Take back control, take back what you own rightfully at your birth right which is the power of your thought, your body and your mind!

Change is never made easy, but yet it is one of the ultimate things a person can do and it can be done. A person can change himself by simply change his level of thinking thoughts. By thinking of those trivial issues does not significantly increase the level and degree of the persons thinking. But rather think about bigger issues which really stretches the mind.

Sow a thought, reap an action. Sow an action, reap a habit. Sow a habit, reap a character. Sow a character, reap a destiny. It is all repetition, until you have embodied these chapters into your life. Take some time to digest all these information, embody them and finally, become the dying breed, by becoming what who you really are, and what you really are. You are who you are by understanding what went in and out of your mind.

After reading this book, the reader got to consciously decide how does this book impact on the reader, is it positively or negatively with an open mind? Things and the environment will not change unless something changes and you are supposed to make the change. To make the necessary changes, note, it has to be willing/ own accord and own deliberate decision to make that change. The choice is yours and I know you can and will make a good choice. Do not study other people, but rather learn and study more of yourself because you are unique and special and you are the only 1 of you in the world!

The end of the book is actually the new beginning of your life chapter, spent time to think because what comes before action? It is your thoughts that comes before action and spent some quality time thinking, think big and be big because you are unstoppable, it is in all of our blood!

Printed in the United States
By Bookmasters